Ooey-Gooey Animals

Jellyfish

Lola M. Schaefer

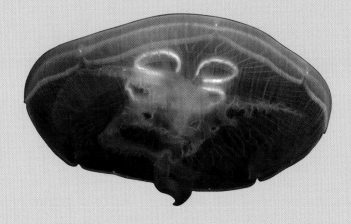

Heinemann Library
Chicago, Illinois

© 2002 Reed Educational & Professional Publishing
Published by Heinemann Library,
an imprint of Reed Educational & Professional Publishing,
Chicago, Illinois

Customer Service 888-454-2279
Visit our website at www.heinemannlibrary.com

Designed by Suzanne Emerson/Heinemann Library and Ginkgo Creative, Inc.
Printed and bound in the U.S.A. by Lake Book

06 05 04 03 02
10 9 8 7 6 5 4 3 2 1

Library of Congress Cataloging-in-Publication Data
Schaefer, Lola M., 1950-
   Jellyfish / Lola Schaefer.
        p. cm. — (Ooey-gooey animals)
Includes index.
Summary: An introduction to jellyfish, discussing their habitat, food,
physical features, and activities.
   ISBN 1-58810-505-9 (HC), 1-58810-714-0 (Pbk.)
   1. Jellyfishes—Juvenile literature. [1. Jellyfishes.] I. Title.
   QL377.S4 S33 2002
   593.5'3—dc21

                          2001003005

Acknowledgments
The author and publishers are grateful to the following for permission to reproduce copyright material:
Title page, pp. 5, 17 Brandon D. Cole/Corbis; pp. 4, 18 Index Stock Imagery, Inc.; p. 6 Stephen Frink/Corbis; pp. 7, 9, 11, 15 Wernher Krutein/Photovault; p. 8 W. Wayne Lockwood, M.D./Corbis; p. 9 Photovault; p. 10 Cordaiy Photo Library Ltd./Corbis; p. 12L Jeffrey L. Rotman/Corbis; p. 12R Kim Saar/Heinemann Library; p. 13 Howard Hall/HHP; p. 14 Corbis; p. 16 Amos Nachoum/Corbis; p. 19 Norbert Wu Photography; p. 20 Karen Gowlett-Holmes; p. 21 Peter Parks/IQ-3D/Mo Yung Productions/Norbert Wu Photography; p. 22 Photovault

Cover photograph courtesy of Brandon D. Cole/Corbis

Every effort has been made to contact copyright holders of any material reproduced in this book. Any omissions will be rectified in subsequent printings if notice is given to the publisher.

Special thanks to our advisory panel for their help in the preparation of this book:

Eileen Day, Preschool Teacher
Chicago, IL

Paula Fischer, K–1 Teacher
Indianapolis, IN

Sandra Gilbert,
Library Media Specialist
Houston, TX

Angela Leeper,
Educational Consultant
North Carolina Department
of Public Instruction
Raleigh, NC

Pam McDonald,
Reading Teacher
Winter Springs, FL

Melinda Murphy,
Library Media Specialist
Houston, TX

Helen Rosenberg, MLS
Chicago, IL

Anna Marie Varakin,
Reading Instructor
Western Maryland College

Special thanks to Dr. Randy Kochevar of the Monterey Bay Aquarium for his help in the preparation of this book.

Some words are shown in bold, **like this.**
You can find them in the picture glossary on page 23.

Contents

What Are Jellyfish?

Jellyfish are animals without bones.

They are **invertebrates**.

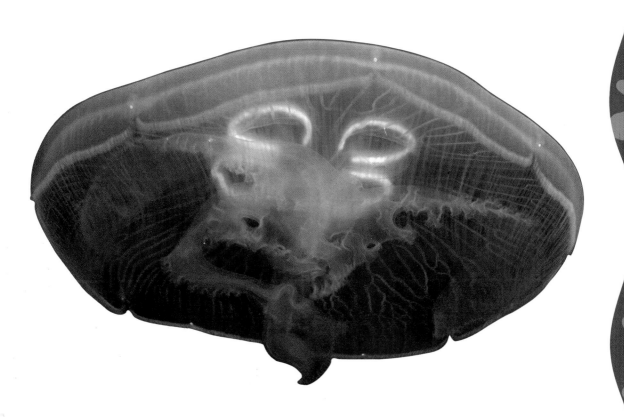

Jellyfish bodies are filled with **gel**.

Gel is clear and watery.

Where Do Jellyfish Live?

All jellyfish live in water.

Most jellyfish live in oceans.

Jellyfish live in cold and warm water.

They can live close to land or in deep water.

What Do Jellyfish Look Like?

Jellyfish can be clear or colorful.

Jellyfish bodies are called **bells.**

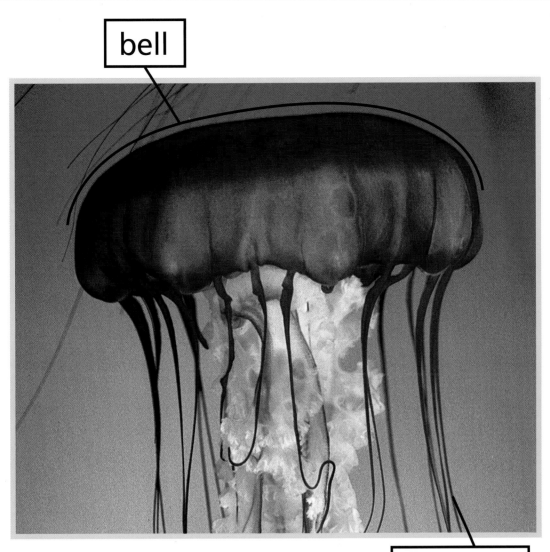

bell

tentacle

Bells look like umbrellas or bubbles.

Tentacles hang from the bell.

What Do Jellyfish Feel Like?

mucus

Jellyfish feel soft and gooey.

There is **mucus** on the outside of their bodies.

tentacle

People do not often touch jellyfish.

Some jellyfish **tentacles** can sting!

How Big Are Jellyfish?

Some jellyfish **bells** are very big.

But some are as small as pennies.

Jellyfish **tentacles** can be very long.

These tentacles are longer than this diver!

How Do Jellyfish Move?

Jellyfish move by taking water into their **bells**.

Then, they push the water out.

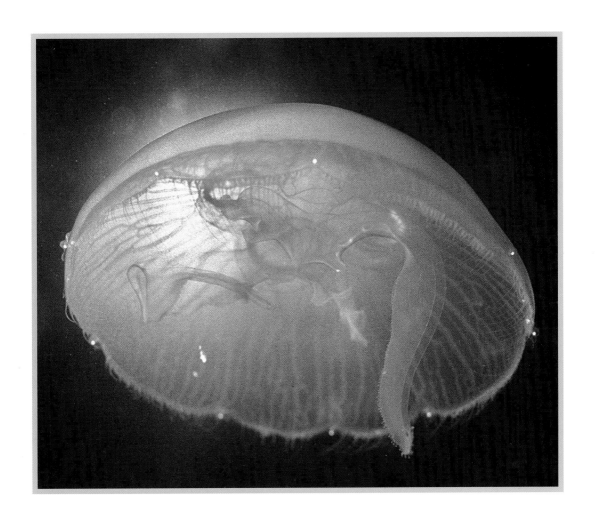

Waves can move jellyfish, too.

What Do Jellyfish Do All Day?

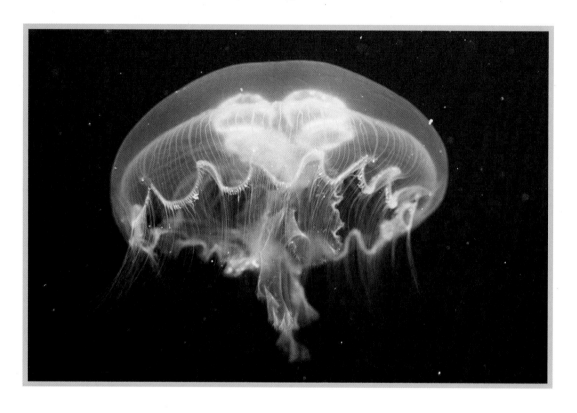

Jellyfish swim through the water.

They are always hunting for food.

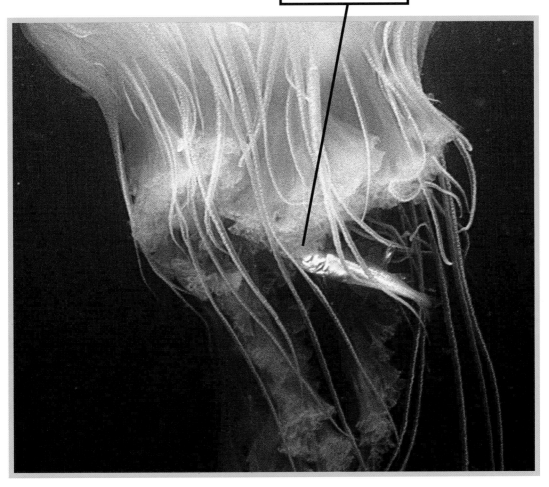

mouth

Jellyfish have mouths under their **bells.**

Their **tentacles** bring food to their mouths.

What Do Jellyfish Eat?

Jellyfish eat other animals in the ocean.

They eat small animals and fish.

They sting animals with their
tentacles.

Then, they eat them.

Where Do New Jellyfish Come From?

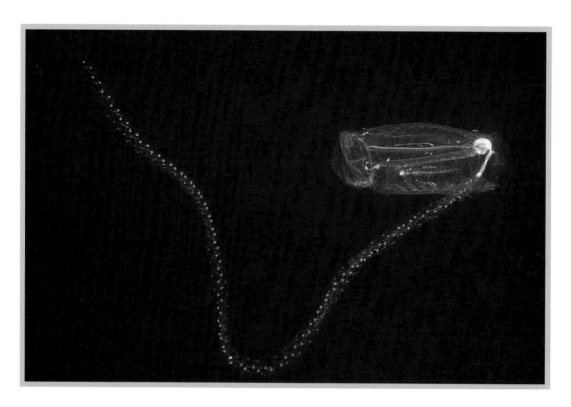

Adult jellyfish lay eggs in the water.

The eggs grow into small animals.

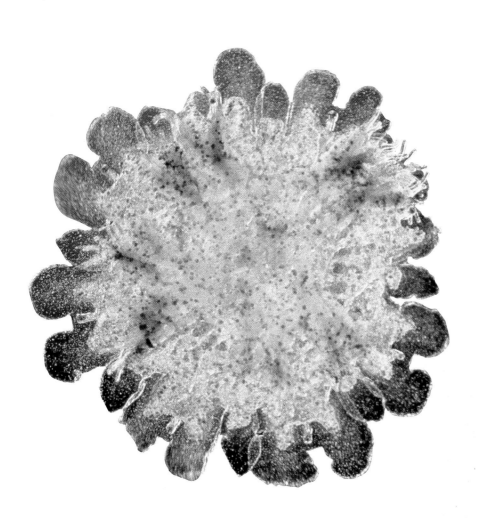

These animals grow round shapes.

The round shapes break off and grow into jellyfish.

Quiz

What are these jellyfish parts?

Can you find them in the book?

Look for the answers on page 24.

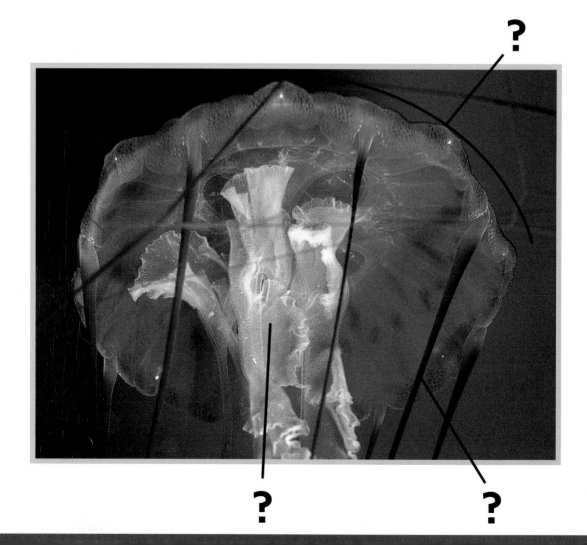

Picture Glossary

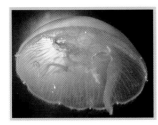
bell
pages
8, 9, 12, 14,
17

mucus
(MYOO-kus)
page 10

gel
page 5

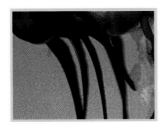
tentacles
(TEN-tah-kuls)
pages
9, 11, 13, 17, 19

invertebrate
(in-VUR-tuh-brate)
page 4

Note to Parents and Teachers

Reading for information is an important part of a child's literacy development. Learning begins with a question about something. Help children think of themselves as investigators and researchers by encouraging their questions about the world around them. Each chapter in this book begins with a question. Read the question together. Look at the pictures. Talk about what you think the answer might be. Then read the text to find out if your predictions were correct. Think of other questions you could ask about the topic, and discuss where you might find the answers. Assist children in using the picture glossary and the index to practice new vocabulary and research skills.

! CAUTION: Remind children that it is not a good idea to handle wild animals. Children should wash their hands with soap and water after they touch any animal.

Index

Answers to quiz on page 22

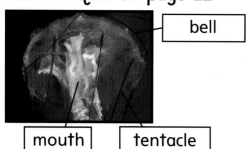

bell
mouth
tentacle

24